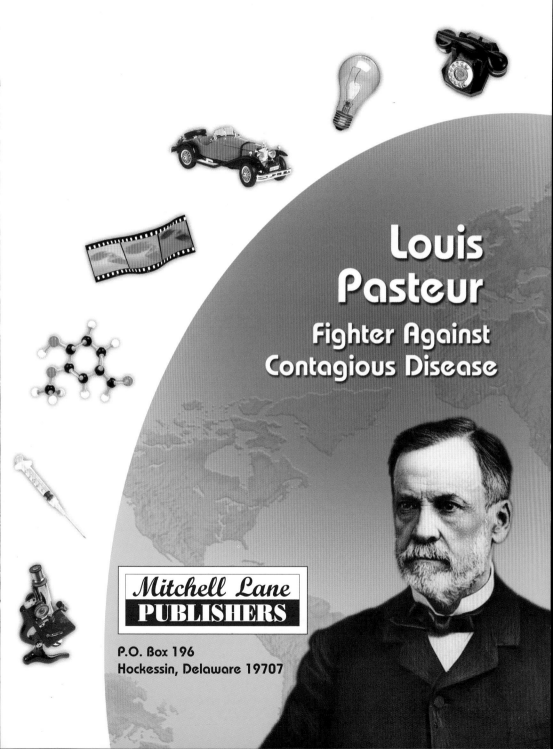

Uncharted, Unexplored, and Unexplained

Scientific Advancements of the 19th Century

Louis Pasteur

Fighter Against Contagious Disease

Mitchell Lane
PUBLISHERS

P.O. Box 196
Hockessin, Delaware 19707

Uncharted, Unexplored, and Unexplained

Scientific Advancements of the 19th Century

Visit us on the web: www.mitchelllane.com
Comments? email us: mitchelllane@mitchelllane.com

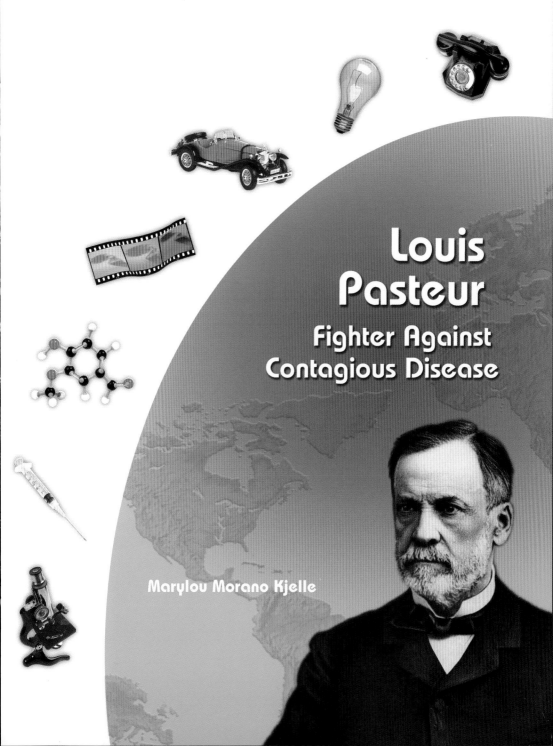

Uncharted, Unexplored, and Unexplained

Scientific Advancements of the 19th Century

Louis Pasteur

Fighter Against Contagious Disease

Marylou Morano Kjelle

Uncharted, Unexplored, and Unexplained

Scientific Advancements of the 19th Century

Copyright © 2005 by Mitchell Lane Publishers, Inc. All rights reserved. No part of this book may be reproduced without written permission from the publisher. Printed and bound in the United States of America.

Printing 1   2   3   4   5   6   7   8
Library of Congress Cataloging-in-Publication Data
Kjelle, Marylou Morano.
Louis Pasteur / by Marylou Morano Kjelle.
     p. cm. — (Uncharted, unexplored, and unexplained scientific advancements of
     the 19th century)
    Includes bibliographical references and index.
ISBN 1-58415-363-6 (library bound)
1. Pasteur, Louis, 1822-1895. 2. Microbiologists—France—Biography—Juvenile literature.
I.Title. II. Uncharted, unexplored & unexplained.
QR31.P37K56 2005
509.2—dc22

2004024616

ABOUT THE AUTHOR: Marylou Morano Kjelle is a freelance writer and photojournalist who lives and works in central New Jersey. She is a regular contributor to several local newspaper and online publications. Marylou writes a column for the *Westfield Leader/Times of Scotch Plains—Fanwood* called "Children's Book Nook," where she reviews children's books. She has written thirteen nonfiction books for young readers and co-authored and edited others. Marylou has a M.S. degree in Science from Rutgers University and teaches both science and writing at a community college in New Jersey.

PHOTO CREDITS: Cover, pp. 1, 3, 6—Getty Images; p. 8—Corbis; pp. 9, 10—Pasteur College; pp. 12, 18—Getty Images; p. 20—Hulton/Archive; p. 22—Corbis; p. 26—Getty Images; pp. 30, 35—Corbis; p. 38—Getty Images; p. 41—Corbis

PUBLISHER'S NOTE: This story is based on the author's extensive research, which she believes to be accurate. Documentation of such research is contained on page 47.

The internet sites referenced herein were active as of the publication date. Due to the fleeting nature of some web sites, we cannot guarantee they will all be active when you are reading this book.

Uncharted, Unexplored, and Unexplained
Scientific Advancements of the 19th Century

Louis Pasteur
Fighter Against Contagious Disease

*For Your Information

Dr. Louis Pasteur, the father of modern bacteriology and pioneer of the treatment of numerous diseases by vaccination, became interested in rabies at the age of nine. At that time, a rabid wolf stormed out of the woods near his home village of Arbois, France, and bit eight people. Pasteur never forgot the sounds of the victims' screams as their wounds were cauterized – the only known treatment for rabies at the time.

1

A Prepared Mind

Louis Pasteur stood quietly in his lab, listening to the howls and growls echoing off the walls of the animal room. He knew the demonic sounds were coming from dogs infected with rabies. Although he could not see the animals, he knew all too well how they looked. They were fierce creatures with snapping jaws and foaming green saliva dripping from their mouths.

The year was 1884, and sixty-one-year-old Pasteur was studying the disease. It was caused by a virus that attacks the central nervous system. In humans rabies is also called hydrophobia, a word that means "fear of water." One of the symptoms infected humans endure is being unable to swallow their own saliva. Victims also twitch and convulse and are startled by the slightest sound.

Pasteur had been interested in rabies since he was nine years old and a rabid wolf stormed out of the woods and into the town of Arbois. The wolf bit eight people. At the time, the only known way to prevent rabies from an animal bite was to cauterize the bite—to burn it with a hot iron poker. Often this "medical treatment" did not work and the person died a painful death. No one understood why burning sometimes worked and sometimes didn't. The only thing that was clear was that patients who were bitten and who were not cauterized always died. After all these years, Pasteur could still remember that long-ago day, and the sounds of the victims' screams as their wounds were cauterized.

Pasteur had proven that an animal could become immune to a particular disease by becoming exposed to a weak version of it. Intentional exposure to a weak strain is called vaccination. In 1881, at Pouilly-le-Fort, Pasteur had successfully tested a vaccine—an injection of weakened bacteria—against a disease of cattle called anthrax. Now he was working on a vaccine against rabies. He knew that if he injected the green saliva from a rabid dog into another animal, the second animal would get rabies. He also knew that an animal could be given rabies by having the infected material injected directly into its brain. Pasteur infected one animal, then injected another with infected material from the first. In this way he passed the virus from dog to monkey to

Robert Koch was a German-born scientist who studied a disease of cattle called anthrax. Koch determined that spores that had been dormant for a number of years could develop the rod-shaped bacteria that caused anthrax. It was only after Pasteur's development of an anthrax vaccine that Koch's work received recognition.

rabbit to guinea pig. Each time the virus was passed from one animal to the next, it became weaker. Pasteur was looking to find a vaccine that was strong enough to be recognized by the animal's body, but too weak to cause rabies.

Through experimentation, Pasteur discovered the correct strength of vaccine that would prevent rabies in dogs. The vaccine had to be given before symptoms developed. He had given the disease, and then the vaccine before symptoms developed, to fifty dogs. All fifty had been resistant to rabies without a single failure. Now all that remained was to try the vaccine on humans. In March of 1885, Louis was thinking of trying the vaccine on himself. "I . . . can render [dogs] immune to rabies after they have been bitten by mad dogs. I have not yet dared treat humans bitten by rabid dogs. But . . . I seriously think of starting with myself . . . so sure [I am] of my results," he wrote to his friend Jules Vercel.[1]

Before he could test the vaccine on himself, however, a nine-year-old boy named Joseph Meister and his mother arrived at Pasteur's lab. The boy had been bitten fourteen times by a rabid dog. With the two was the dog's owner, who had killed the dog. The boy's mother begged Pasteur to save her son's life by giving him the vaccine. Pasteur hesitated. He knew the vaccine worked on dogs. He was sure it would work on himself. But could he inject young Joseph Meister with a vaccine that had never before been tried on humans? Would it do more harm than good?

Pasteur consulted with other doctors who convinced him to try it. Without the vaccine, the boy would surely die. With it, he at least had a chance.

Pasteur's success can be credited, in part, to his strong work ethic. Pasteur believed that hard work led to success. Here he is working in his lab, surrounded by lab animals in their cages.

9

This is a picture of Louis Pasteur giving a vaccination to a young boy. The first human to receive the rabies vaccine was nine-year-old Joseph Meister, who had been bitten fourteen times by a rabid dog. Young Joseph received a dose of vaccine every day for ten days, a protocol that saved his life.

Pasteur injected Joseph with a small piece of spinal cord from a rabid rabbit. Each day for ten more days, he injected a small amount of the material into the boy. Each day's injection was a stronger form of the virus to build up the boy's resistance. Pasteur constantly observed the boy for signs of rabies, but Joseph remained healthy. The vaccine had prevented the dreaded disease. Word spread, and in the following weeks, Pasteur and his coworkers inoculated three hundred and fifty people. In only one instance did the vaccine fail to prevent the disease. "Chance favors the prepared mind," Pasteur was fond of saying. His prepared mind helped the world conquer rabies, and many other diseases as well.

Rabies

Rabies is most common in dogs and cats.

The word rabies comes from the Latin word meaning "madness." The disease is caused by a rhabdovirus, a virus that is shaped like a bullet. Seven to eight thousand cases of rabies are diagnosed in domestic and wild animals each year in the United States. Skunks, bats, raccoons, foxes, and coyotes are all known to get rabies, but it is most common in dogs and cats.

The rabies virus is found in the saliva of an infected animal. Humans can get the virus if they are bitten or licked by an animal with the disease. Less than ten cases of human rabies are reported in the United States each year. The virus enters a cut, scratch, or skin broken by the bite. It multiplies in muscles and other parts of the body near the site of the bite. Then the virus travels through the nerves to the spinal chord and then to the brain. The virus causes damage to the nerves of the brain and spinal chord and eventually causes death.

One of the symptoms of rabies is anxiety. Another is twitching of the muscles of the mouth and throat. The twitching usually occurs when an infected person feels an air draft or sees water.

Rabies is an unusual disease because it has an incubation period of weeks or months. An incubation period is the period of time that passes between being bitten and showing symptoms of the disease. It is the time during which the virus is "incubating," and getting ready to do its damage. The long incubation time gives the rabies vaccine the chance to protect against the disease. This protection is called immunity. The vaccine causes the body to activate special white blood cells called antibodies. The rabies antibodies then fight the rabies virus and stop the disease and its symptoms.

Pasteur's original rabies vaccine was created by drying the brain and spinal chord tissue of infected rabbits. Today the vaccine is prepared in a laboratory using chick embryo cells or human cells. In 1885, Pasteur gave Joseph Meister a series of ten shots. Today the vaccine is given in six shots. Neither Pasteur's vaccine, nor the vaccines used today contain active rabies virus. Therefore the vaccines can not cause rabies.

Joseph Meister was just nine years old when he became the first human to be successfully inoculated against rabies. Meister remained associated with the Pasteur Institute virtually all of his life. Like Pasteur, Meister was a fiercely patriotic person; legend has it that Joseph Meister committed suicide, when the Germans invaded France in 1940.

2

A Boy in Arbois

Hanging on the walls of the Pasteur Institute in Paris are portraits painted by the man after whom the institute is named. Louis Pasteur, the scientist who brought about a revolution in medicine, public health, and microbiology, might have instead become a painter. Long after Pasteur had made a name for himself in the world of science, an art critic wrote, "No one will regret that Pasteur chose a scientific career. But, if he had wanted to, he would have held his own among the painters and—who knows?—become a very great painter."[1]

Yes, who knows? What might our lives be like today had young Louis been encouraged to attend art school instead of college? What might the world be like now if he had chosen the life of an artist over that of a scientist?

Louis's parents, Jean-Joseph and Jeanne Pasteur, had neither art nor science in mind for their only son. They wanted him to become a teacher. There had never been a teacher in the family before. The first Pasteurs had been shepherds. Jean-Joseph, however, had followed in the footsteps of his more recent forefathers and become a tanner. Although Jean-Joseph had been orphaned as a child, his aunts had made sure he learned the family trade.

Jean-Joseph was a serious and quiet man. It may have been the loss of his parents that made him so serious. Or maybe it was the years he spent as a soldier in the Third Regiment of the French Army, serving under Napoléon Bonaparte. For his bravery, Jean-Joseph had received the Ribbon of the Legion of Honor from the emperor himself. He was so proud of this award, he never left his home without the red ribbon pinned to his overcoat.

Louis's mother, Jeanne-Étiennette Roqui, was the daughter of a gardener. She had a cheerful personality that balanced Jean-Joseph's quiet one. After their marriage in 1816, Jean-Joseph and Jeanne moved to the ancient French village of Dole on the Doubs River, a short distance from the France-Switzerland border. There Jean-Joseph set up a tannery, and Jeanne began having children. The Pasteurs had one son who died before his first birthday, and a daughter, Jeanne-Antoine, whom they called Virginie, before Louis was born on December 27, 1822. Two more daughters, Josephine and Emilie, came after Louis. Emilie was stricken by a fever when she was three years old. It left her mentally disabled.

By the time Louis was five years old, the Pasteurs were living in Arbois, a pretty town on the Cuisance River known for its vineyards. Jean-Joseph set up another tannery, and the family moved into a set of rooms over the work area. The Pasteurs were a close and loving family. They were devout Catholics who were actively involved in their community. Louis enjoyed a normal childhood in Arbois. Like other boys his age, he preferred fishing for trout to going to school. He played marbles and capture-the-flag with the sons of vintners, who were his friends. The boys ice-skated on the Cuisance River in the winter and swam in its refreshing waters in the summer. And all year they eagerly awaited the autumn wine harvest where, after picking the grapes, the entire town would celebrate with food, wine, and festivities.

Louis's early academic reports show no indication of the scientific genius he was to become. His teachers at the lycée (lower school) labeled him a "slow" student. "Had he been subjected to the intelligence tests that nowadays are employed to determine the mental alertness of children, he certainly would have been classed as one of the slowest," wrote Pasteur Vallery-Radot, Louis's grandson, more than one hundred years later.[2]

Jean-Joseph, having only the most basic education himself, helped Louis with his studies as best as he could. He enjoyed telling Louis about the days he spent serving in the army. His stories about Napoléon's military conquests inspired national pride in his son, and the younger Pasteur remained passionately patriotic all his life. "In teaching me to read, you made sure that I learned about the greatness of France," Louis once told his father.[3]

By the time he was in ninth grade, Louis, with the help of a tutor, had begun to apply himself to his studies and was winning academic awards. Monsieur Romanet, the headmaster of the Collège d'Arbois, recognized Louis's potential and encouraged him to apply to the École Normale Supérieure, a prestigious college in Paris. Paris was France's intellectual center. The École Normale prepared promising students for positions as university professors.

Monsieur Romanet's encouragement made Jean-Joseph a little uneasy. He had high ambitions for Louis, but they were not that high. No need to study in Paris when the college in nearby Besançon would do. And why should Louis become a university professor? Teaching in the lycée or becoming a headmaster at the Collège d'Arbois was plenty ambitious for the son of a tanner.

In the end, Monsieur Romanet won the argument. Louis would attend École Normale. To prepare for admission, Louis enrolled in Lycée Saint-Louis, a preparatory school located in Paris's Latin Quarter. In 1838, when he was fifteen years old, Louis and his good friend Jules Vercel made the two-hundred-mile trip from Arbois to Paris by stagecoach.

The Lycée Saint-Louis was run by Monsieur Barbet, and Louis and Jules boarded with the Barbet family. Jules had no trouble adapting, but Louis became homesick shortly after the boys' arrival. He missed his own close family and small town. At times he was so depressed that he was unable to study. "Oh, if I only could get a whiff of the old tannery I feel that I would be all right," he said to Jules.[4] Unable to help Louis, and alarmed by his state of mind, Monsieur Barbet contacted Jean-Joseph. One month after Louis's arrival, Jean-Joseph traveled to Paris to collect his son and bring him back to Arbois.

Jean-Joseph asked no questions of Louis during the long trip home. Louis felt shame and embarrassment over being unable able to stay in Paris, but reasoned it was not totally his fault. Part of the blame lay with his father and Monsieur Romanet. They had expected too much of him by sending him away to school, and the adults agreed with Louis. Their shouldering of some of the responsibility helped Louis repair his damaged self-esteem.

After returning from Paris, Louis went back to the Collège d'Arbois. He remained there until 1839 and completed all the required courses for graduation. He did well academically. He also continued to paint and draw, and he performed in the school's production of Molière's *Le Misanthrope,* playing the part of Alceste.

When it was time once again to enroll at École Normale, Louis found that he lacked one required course for admission—philosophy. In 1839, he moved to Besançon, about thirty miles from Arbois, to study philosophy at the Collège Royal de Besançon. This time there was no homesickness. Besançon was not as far from Arbois as Paris. Louis would be able to see his father often, as Jean-Joseph traveled to Besançon several times a year to sell hides at a leather fair.

By this time, both of Louis's parents had realized that their son's potential far exceeded that of being a teacher or headmaster in a small local college. While a student at Besançon, Louis and his family remained close, and through letters, his sisters eagerly followed each step of their brother's career. An only son, Louis felt it was his duty to advise his parents on his sisters' education, and offered to take on extra tutoring so that Josephine could continue her studies at a boarding school. To his sisters he wrote: "I urge you to work hard and love one another . . . work is the foundation of everything in this world. . . it nearly always leads to success."[5]

At Besançon, Louis studied philosophy, math, and physical science. Although he did well in all subjects, he was always striving to do better. He was studious, reserved, and did not socialize with the other students. Most of his time was consumed by schoolwork. Studying in the evening by candlelight caused him eyestrain and headaches. "The final exam has given me a truly fine headache," he wrote home, adding, "Actually this happens whenever we have an exam."[6] To break the tension caused by his studies, Louis spent time with Charles Chappuis, a classmate who would become a lifelong friend and confidant. And Louis's paintings, which he created in his leisure time, were in great demand by fellow students. The paintings earned him the nickname "the Artist."

Louis was awarded a bachelor of letters degree in August 1840. His final grades were "good" in all subjects except elementary science, in which he was considered "very good." He immediately began studying for a bachelor of science degree, a requirement for entering École Normale. The Collège Royal de Besançon helped Louis financially by making him "monitor of supplementary studies." For this position, he tutored other students while he prepared for his own examinations. In return he received room and board and a stipend of 25 francs per month. He used the money to purchase firewood, candles, and food.

Louis failed the first time he took the examinations for the bachelor of science. He remained at Besançon for a second year of classes in advanced mathematics. In 1841 he wrote his parents, "Nothing dries up the heart like this study of mathematics: it makes one lose all sensitivity."[7]

Louis found the second examinations "a hundred times more difficult," yet he passed, and in 1842 he received a bachelor of science degree. In an ironic twist, the student who was to become one of the greatest chemists of all time received a mere "mediocre" for his grade in chemistry.

Napoleon Bonaparte

Napoleon Bonaparte, also known as Napoleon I, was born on the island of Corsica on August 15, 1769. When he was ten years old, his father enrolled him in a military school in Brienne, France, where he stayed until he was fifteen years old. His first army assignment was as second lieutenant, but he quickly moved up the ranks. The execution of the French monarchy during the Revolution caused many European nations to turn hostile to France. During the late 1700s and early 1800s, France was constantly at war. As army commander, Napoleon led his country in victory against Britain, Austria, and the Turks.

Napoleon Bonaparte

In November 1799, the French army overthrew the government. A consulate (a form of government overseen by consuls or chief magistrates) was formed and Napoleon named himself the first consul. Later he was named Consul for Life as well as Emperor of France. Napoleon reorganized French laws and schools. He supported the arts, education, and the sciences, and in general improved life for French citizens. Napoleon's legal system was called Code Napoleon.

In 1803, Britain again declared war on France. This was the beginning of the Napoleonic Wars. Napoleon made elaborate plans to invade England. When Austria and Russia sided with Britain, Napoleon fought them first. He defeated the Austrian troops and made his brothers kings of Naples and Holland. With land won from Austria, Napoleon formed a Confederation of the Rhine. Napoleon then went on to defeat Prussia (which had sided with his enemies) and Russia. Each defeat brought new lands under Napoleon's control and increased the size of his empire. Napoleon, however, never did invade England.

In 1807 Napoleon invaded Portugal and named his brother king of Spain. The Portuguese people rebelled. This started the five year long Peninsular War. Pasteur's father, Jean-Joseph was a soldier in the Third Regiment in northern Spain during the Peninsular War.

In 1812, the year the British invaded the United States capital of Washington, D.C., Napoleon declared war on Russia. All of Europe united against Napoleon and in 1814, he was defeated. Napoleon was exiled to the Island of Elba. Not one to stay down, by 1815, he had raised an army and marched into Belgium. He was defeated at the Battle of Waterloo on June 18, 1815. Once again he was exiled. He died on St. Helena, an island in the Atlantic Ocean on May 5, 1821.

17

At École Normale, Pasteur was a studious young man who often studied twelve hours a day. On Sundays he visited the laboratory of well-known chemist Jean-Baptiste Dumas. It was Dumas who inspired young Pasteur to pursue a career as a chemist.

3

A Chemist by Training

Once he had his bachelor of science degree, Pasteur took the entrance exam for École Normale and was accepted. However, his perfectionist nature emerged and he turned down his acceptance. He had ranked number fifteen out of twenty-two applicants on his entrance exam, and was not pleased with his standing. He returned to Paris to live with the Barbets and study once again at the Lycée Saint-Louis. His friend Chappuis was already in Paris studying at École Normale. His presence helped Pasteur stave off homesickness. When Pasteur took the entrance examination the second time in 1843, he placed fourth in his class. He began his studies at École Normale later that year.

At École Normale, Pasteur studied twelve hours a day. Although physics was his major course, he began attending the lectures of the best-known chemist in France at the time, Jean-Baptiste Dumas, a professor at the Sorbonne, the University of Paris. Dumas, who presented his lectures dressed in a black suit, white vest, and black tie, could, according to Pasteur, "set fire to the soul."[1] Dumas was a member of the Academy of Sciences and had founded the Central School of Arts and Manufacturing to train prospective engineers. Pasteur wrote to Dumas, introducing himself and requesting a position as his teaching assistant. Dumas could not offer Pasteur a position, but he did take note of the young science student. From that point on, Dumas took an active interest in Pasteur's work.

One of the skills Pasteur learned was glass blowing. This came in handy in later years when he needed special glassware for the experiments he designed. Here a man demonstrates the art of glass blowing.

Pasteur spent many hours in the chemistry laboratory, where in addition to scientific experimentation, he learned wood lathing and planning, and glass blowing. These skills would be helpful to him in his laboratory. His free time was spent studying in the library, and on Sunday afternoons he observed experimentation in Dumas's laboratory at the Sorbonne.

In 1844 Pasteur began to study crystallography, the science of crystals. Crystals are the hardened form of a substance. Pasteur was curious about a chemical mystery that chemists had been studying for over twenty years. Tartaric acid, a crusty substance that grows naturally on the inside of wine barrels and on grapes, had been discovered by a Swedish chemist named Carl Wilhelm Scheele. Paratartaric (also called racemic) acid, a similar substance, had been produced accidentally fifty years later by a French industrialist. The two acids had been studied extensively by a German chemist, Eilhardt Mitscherlich, and a French crystallographer, Jean-Baptiste Biot. Neither scientist had been able to find any difference in the physical or chemical properties of the two acids.

Pasteur believed there was a difference between tartaric acid and paratartaric acids. At the time, crystallography was closely associated with research in optics, the study of light. When a beam of polarized light is passed through a substance, the substance will rotate the light to either the left or right. Pasteur was aware of the value of optics as an experimental tool. Building upon Biot's observations, Pasteur designed experiments that showed that although they were identical in their crystalline forms, tartaric and paratartaric acids demonstrated different reactions when subjected to beams of polarized light. The tartaric acid reacted by rotating the light to the right. The paratartaric acid had no reaction—it was optically inactive.

Pasteur wondered why two identical crystalline substances showed such a difference in their reaction to polarized light. The problem had no practical application—it was a problem of pure, not applied, science. But that didn't lessen its importance to Pasteur, who felt the acquisition of any scientific knowledge was significant. He wanted to study science and discover answers for the sake of science itself. Uncovering the reason tartaric and paratartaric acid reacted differently to polarized light could quite possibly clarify or explain some other unsolved scientific mystery. "When I began to pursue specific research, I sought to strengthen my abilities by studying crystals, anticipating that this would provide me with knowledge I could use in the study of chemistry," Pasteur said.[2]

Attending lectures at École Normale and preparing for his doctoral exams took up much of Pasteur's time, but he never stopped thinking about the tartaric-paratartaric question. Over the years, when he had time to devote to his own research, he observed what previous investigators had overlooked: Both the tartaric and paratartaric crystals contained tiny facets, or scratches on their surface. The tartaric acid crystals had facets facing only on one side, while the paratartaric crystals contained a mixture of facets that faced both right and left. Pasteur separated paratartaric right-facing facets from its left-facing facets and prepared solutions of each.

In 1820, British scientist Sir John Herschel had shown that quartz samples whose facets point in the same direction rotate polarized light in that direction. Basing his own research on Herschel's discovery, Pasteur hypothesized that the solution of right-facing crystals would reflect polarized light to the right, and the left-facing crystals would reflect it to the left. Using a polarimeter, an instrument invented by Biot that measures light, Pasteur proved his hypothesis correct. In addition, when there were equal amounts of both facets present in the paratartaric crystals solution, there was no overall effect on the light. The right-facing facets and the left-facing facets canceled each other out.

While some scientists were amazed at Pasteur's discovery, many were skeptical. The French Academy of Sciences asked Biot to verify Pasteur's results. Upon doing so, the older scientist grabbed Pasteur's arm and exclaimed, "My son, I am so deeply in love with science that this makes my heart beat faster."[3] Biot thought so highly of Pasteur and his crystal research that he began to think of himself as Pasteur's mentor, and of Pasteur as an adoptive son.

Pasteur's study of crystals opened up a new branch of science called stereochemistry, the science of the arrangement and position of particles in space.

After obtaining a Ph.D. in science from École Normale Supérieure in 1847, Pasteur turned down an appointment as physics teacher at the college of Tournon. He wanted to remain at École Normale as a *préparateur* (laboratory assistant) in chemistry. On New Year's Day 1848, Pasteur received a rare letter from his mother. "I think how happy it has made me to have a child who has gone so far, and who enjoys his position so much . . ."[4] By this time, Pasteur was charting a course that bypassed his parents' original goals for him

In 1820, British scientist Sir John Herschel showed that quartz samples whose facets (scratches) point in the same direction rotate polarized light in that direction. Pasteur based his own crystal studies on Herschel's research.

of becoming a teacher in a lycée. He had set his sights on a position as a university professor, where he could conduct research as well as teach. "Of all the candidates, you are the only one who can give a lecture," commented one of his teachers at École Normale.[5] Pasteur agreed with his professor's observation and wrote to Chappuis, "We who are called professors should first of all be able to do a good job in teaching."[6]

One of the advantages of the *préparateur* position was that it allowed Pasteur to continue his own research. While working in the laboratory of Antoine-Jérôme Balard—who in 1826 had discovered bromine—Pasteur was introduced to Auguste Laurent, professor of chemistry at the University of Bordeaux. Laurent had completed extensive work in crystallography. While his association with Laurent was brief, the experienced researcher instilled in Pasteur the importance of crystalline forms in understanding chemical analysis. This was a thesis Pasteur would carry with him into his future research.

National unrest rocked Paris in February 1848. The unpopular king Louis-Philippe was overthrown, and a Republic with a provisional government was formed. At first, Pasteur's ability to focus on research allowed him to ignore the constant rioting in the streets. In April, however, he joined the National Guard and did his part to maintain civilian law and order. The guardsmen were "full of spirit and ready to defend the Republic and to restore the respect for order," Pasteur wrote to his father.[7]

Pasteur was called away from his research again later in 1848 when he received a message from Arbois that his mother was ill. Jeanne had suffered a cerebral hemorrhage and died before he arrived. Pasteur blamed himself for her death. He believed worrying about him in riot-torn Paris had contributed to her illness. To ease his guilt, Pasteur offered to leave Paris and move closer to home to assist his father with the care of his younger sisters.

Resigning his position at École Normale, Pasteur accepted a professorship of physics at a lycée in Dijon, close to Arbois. Although sympathetic to his students' needs, his heart remained at École Normale, and his ambitions on crystalline research. He had already published a paper entitled "Report on the Relationship Between the Crystalline Form, the Chemical Composition and the Directory of Rotary Polarization." At the age of twenty-six, Pasteur was one of the leading scientists in Europe.

When a position at the University of Strasbourg as assistant professor of chemistry became available in 1849, Pasteur abandoned both his family and his students. He moved to Strasbourg so quickly that he did not even wait for his replacement to arrive at the lycée.

Pasteur adjusted quickly to life in Strasbourg, a center of educational and industrial activity. He taught chemistry and continued his studies on crystals. The location of the university in the area of France known as Alsace pleased him, since he planned to seek industrial uses for his chemical research.

At Strasbourg, Pasteur met Marie Laurent, the twenty-three-year-old daughter of the university rector. She was cheerful and vivacious, yet also kind and humble. Within a month of their meeting, Pasteur had fallen in love with her and proposed marriage. As was the custom at that time, he made his intentions known in a letter to her father. "All that I have to offer," he wrote, is "good health, a good nature, and my position in the University."[8] To Marie, he wrote, "I have only one thought: You. My work no longer means anything to me."[9]

Louis Pasteur and Marie Laurent were married on May 29, 1849. Despite the letter that said his love for Marie was more important than his work, on the morning of the wedding, Pasteur went to the lab as usual. Deep in concentration, his mind on an experiment, he almost missed the ceremony.

Jean-Baptiste Dumas

Jean-Baptiste Dumas

Louis Pasteur and Jean-Baptiste Dumas are two of the greatest scientists of the nineteenth century.

Dumas was born in Alais, France, in 1800. When he was a young man, he went to Geneva to study pharmacy. His early research was not in chemistry, but biology. Dumas became well-known among scientists for his writings on the nervous system. He completed these writings when he was in his 20s. Shortly thereafter, Dumas was asked to come to Paris to teach and carry out research at many schools. In 1829, Dumas started his own school, The Central School of Arts and Manufacturing.

In Paris, Dumas's interests turned to chemistry. He was one of the first scientists to work with alcohols, ethers, and other organic (carbon-containing) compounds. Because of this, Dumas is considered to be one of the founders of organic chemistry. By the time he became a professor of Chemistry at the Sorbonne, Dumas was being called France's first scientist.

Pasteur often visited the Sorbonne to attend Dumas's chemistry classes. Dumas was well-liked by his students. As many as seven hundred would crowd into a large hall at one time to hear him teach. He made chemistry so interesting that attending his lectures was like attending the theatre. And just like the theatre, the students clapped after the lectures to show Dumas how much they enjoyed his classes.

Later in life, Dumas entered politics. He first became a deputy and then a senator. In 1851 he became France's minister of agriculture.

Jean-Baptiste Dumas and his early lectures at the Sorbonne inspired Pasteur's love of chemistry. Over the years Dumas became an important mentor to Pasteur. Even after Dumas was no longer involved in science, Pasteur continued to turn to him for advice. And until his death in 1884, Dumas continued to be interested in Pasteur's work.

"When one is used to working, one cannot longer live without it..." Pasteur once said. Pasteur's wife, Marie, was supportive of Pasteur's work even though it meant he spent long hours away from his home and family. Marie recognized early in their marriage that Pasteur had the potential to be another Newton or Galileo.

4

Wines and Worms

According to Dr. Émile Roux, one of Pasteur's scientific partners, the marriage of Louis and Marie "materialized just to help promote the good things Pasteur was to achieve."[1] From the beginning of their marriage, Marie understood the laboratory came before all else. Roux said: "The first few days of their life together were enough to tell Mme. Pasteur what sort of man she had married. She made it her business to shield him from the practical difficulties of life, assuming responsibility for all household cares and leaving him free to concentrate entirely on research. Her love for him included an understanding of his work. In the evenings she used to write at his dictation; she spurred him to explain himself more clearly; she was genuinely interested. . . . She was not only the ideal wife for him; she was also the best of his scientific collaborators."[2]

By the middle of the 1800s, Pasteur had settled into a comfortable routine of research, teaching, and family. Jeanne, his first daughter, was born in 1850. Next came a son, Jean-Baptiste, who was named after Pasteur's mentor, Jean-Baptiste Biot. Cecile was born in 1853. She was followed by Marie-Louise and Camille.

His supportive wife and his position at the University of Strasbourg enabled Pasteur to concentrate on what was most important to him—his beloved scientific research. By this time he had success with a second chemical discovery: producing racemic acid from tartaric acid. "When one is used to working one can no longer live without it . . . in science one is happy; in science one rises above all others," Pasteur said early on in his career.[3] Of her husband, Marie remarked, "Those [experiments] he is planning for this year are supposed to give us, if they are successful, a Newton or Galileo."[4]

In 1854, thirty-one-year-old Louis was offered the newly created position of dean and professor of chemistry at the University of Lille. Lille was an industrial center in northern France. One of Pasteur's new responsibilities would be to find ways to make science helpful to industry.

One day in late 1856, a distiller named Monsieur Bigo asked Pasteur to study a serious problem that was halting his alcohol production. Alcohol is a product of the manufacture of wine, beer, and some other beverages. It is made from either starch or sugar through the process of fermentation. Monsieur Bigo was fermenting beet juice as the source of his alcohol. But something was going wrong with the fermentation of the sugar beets. Instead of alcohol, a sour-smelling, spoiled liquid was being produced. Monsieur Bigo was just one of many distillers in Lille whose livelihood was being threatened by bad fermentations.

Pasteur did not know much about fermentations, but he set out to learn. He discovered there are several different types of fermentations. The fermentation of the distillers produced alcohol from sugar and starch in grapes, barley, corn, and other plant matter. This type of fermentation is called alcoholic fermentation. The fermentation of wine into vinegar is acetic acid fermentation. The souring of milk is also fermentation—it is called lactic acid fermentation because the sugar in the milk is converted to lactic acid.

Although scientists knew there were different types of fermentations, they did not know much about the actual process itself. The only thing they were sure of was that a microorganism—a tiny life-form that is visible only under a microscope—played a part in fermentation. Yeast is but one of many microorganisms. It is used to ferment fruit or grain and turn it into alcohol during alcoholic fermentation. Without yeast, alcohol would not be produced. Many researchers guessed a type of chemical action caused the sugar, after the yeast had died, to turn into alcohol. Only a few thought it was the yeast themselves that caused the fermentation.

Pasteur drew samples of both good and bad beet juice from Monsieur Bigo's vats. He observed both samples under the microscope. The sample of the good beet juice contained healthy yeast. They were round cells that grew by budding new cells off the old. The spoiled beet juice also contained microorganisms, but these were shaped differently. They were smaller and were long rods instead of circles.

28

Pasteur studied all types of fermentation, including the lactic acid fermentation of sour milk. He concluded that the wrong type of fermentation—the lactic acid fermentation—was occurring in the spoiled beet juice. From this deduction he theorized that each type of fermentation had a different microorganism associated with it. Yeast turned sugar into alcohol. The rodlike microbe found in the spoiled beet juice caused the juice to turn to lactic acid in a lactic acid fermentation.

Pasteur published the results of his lactic acid fermentation research in 1857. In his paper he put forth two groundbreaking theories. The first was that microorganisms caused fermentation. The second was that different microorganisms caused different types of fermentation.

That year, Pasteur was asked by the Minister of Education to become director of scientific studies at École Normale. Pasteur was happy about the appointment and eager to return to Paris. As soon as he was settled in his new laboratory, he began to study spontaneous generation. It was a subject that developed naturally from his fermentation studies. Now that he had discovered that microorganisms caused fermentation, he was curious to learn where they came from. Once he learned this, he could tell distillers like Monsieur Bigo how to keep them out of the vats.

People have always been curious about the origins of living things. The early Greeks and Romans thought life came from dead material. Ancient Greek philosopher Aristotle claimed, "Every dry body which becomes moist and every humid body which dries up breeds life."[5] Through the Middle Ages, scientists theorized that simple life-forms grew spontaneously from nonliving substances in dirt and air. This theory, that nonliving elements give rise to living things, is called spontaneous generation.

For centuries scientists used spontaneous generation to explain the existence of simple life-forms. The invention of the microscope in 1590, however, had scientists rethinking spontaneous generation. As primitive as the early microscopes were, they uncovered an entire new world. The existence of organisms previously unknown made some scientists propose that life came from prior life. This theory was called biogenesis.

Pasteur also believed in biogenesis. "I prefer to think that life comes from life rather than from dust," he said.[6] He hypothesized that the air was full of microscopic organisms that caused contamination in things like vats of beet juice and bowls of broth. These microorganisms multiplied and gave rise to new microorganisms.

29

Spontaneous generation, the theory that life spontaneously arose from nonliving matter, was a popular way of thinking about life that reached back to Aristotle's time. Here is a picture of Aristotle, who lived in the third century B.C., looking at a bust of the poet, Homer, who lived about 500 years earlier. Pasteur disproved Aristotle's belief by showing that life arises from other life, a theory called biogenesis and not spontaneous generation, as Aristotle believed.

In 1858, Pasteur set out to disprove spontaneous generation altogether. He stopped a year later when his oldest daughter, twelve-year-old Jeanne, died of typhoid fever. Deep in grief, Pasteur was for a short while unable to continue his research. Then in the spring of 1860, he began once again to study spontaneous generation. He placed liquid in several flasks and sterilized them by boiling. Then he removed the air from the flasks and sealed them. He took the sterile flasks to several different places. At each location, he opened them briefly so that the outside air mixed with the sterile liquid in the flask. The microorganisms in the air grew in the formerly sterile liquid, clouding it with contamination.

Although the results of his experiments were promising, Pasteur was not completely satisfied. He needed a way to prove that the microorganisms in the air, and not the air itself, were responsible for the cloudy contamination. Antoine-Jérôme Balard, Pasteur's old professor from the École Normale, suggested that Pasteur design a special flask in which to conduct the experiment. Pasteur placed meat broth into a regular flask and sterilized it. He then sterilized the neck of the flask and bent it to resemble an

S, or the neck of a swan. He left the end of the flask open to the air. After a suitable period of time, he checked for growth. There was none. The S shape of the flask trapped the dust and microorganisms present in the air. The microorganisms couldn't reach the broth and multiply. When he cut the flask below the S, letting in the air, the broth was soon teeming with microorganisms. Pasteur called them "invisible giants." Without the trap, the airborne particles had a clear path to the broth, where they could multiply and grow. Pasteur's experiment proved living organisms came from life, and were not spontaneously generated.

Confident he had answered the question of spontaneous generation, Pasteur resumed his studies on fermentation. One day as he was studying a drop of fermenting liquid under the microscope, he observed that not all of the bacteria were moving in the same manner. Some of the bacteria—the ones in the middle of the drop—were actively swimming. But the bacteria near the edges of the drop were motionless. Pasteur hypothesized that oxygen had killed the motionless bacteria. In other words, the bacteria on the edge of the drop were not able to live in the presence of oxygen. Pasteur named these bacteria "anaerobic," from the Greek words that mean "without air."

Pasteur's theory that spontaneous generation did not occur was officially accepted by the French Academy of Science in 1864. "I have kept [the liquid in the S flask] from the only thing man does not know how to produce: from the germs which float in the air, from Life, for Life is a germ and a germ is life. Never will the doctrine of spontaneous generation recover from the mortal blow of this simple experiment," he proclaimed.[7]

Pasteur put all of his new ideas together. His work with fermentation had shown him that germs cause disease. His spontaneous generation experiments had proven that germs were invisible in the air. If air was the source of germs, and germs caused disease, then couldn't disease be spread through the air? Since germs are visible only under a microscope, explained Pasteur, they could be passed unknowingly from one living thing to another. And other things, like water or contaminated bedclothes, could also spread disease.

Pasteur came up with a new theory. He called it the germ theory of disease. The germ theory opened up an entire new way of studying disease and how it is spread. Pasteur's theory is still the basis for what we know about health and illness. Today we acknowledge his germ theory whenever we cover our mouths when coughing or sneezing, or wash our hands before eating. Health care professionals acknowledge the germ theory of disease each time a doctor or dentist puts on a fresh pair of gloves before examining a patient, or sterilizes an instrument before using it during an operation.

Emperor Napoléon III heard of Pasteur's research and was very impressed. He asked Pasteur to study a problem that was affecting the French economy. Something was turning the French wines into acid and changing their flavor. The emperor asked Pasteur to find out why this was happening. Pasteur studied drops of each acidic wine under the microscope. He came to the conclusion that each wine was afflicted by a different microbe, which was causing the wrong type of fermentation.

As had happened so often in his career, just as he was immersing himself in the study of one problem, another came along. The Minister of Agriculture requested he study a disease of silkworms called pebrine, which was also having an impact on the French economy. The cultivation of silkworms was one of France's leading industries, but not only France was affected. Pebrine was killing silkworms throughout the world.

The name *pebrine* had been given to the disease because the infected larvae had brown and black specks that resembled grains of pepper on their bodies. *Pebre* is one way of saying "pepper" in French.

Pasteur knew nothing about silkworms or pebrine, so he began studying. He learned that the disease affects all stages of the silkworm life cycle, from the moth to the egg to the larva to the chrysalis, the silky cocoon of delicate threads which when unraveled were spun into silk.

In June 1865, Pasteur set up a small laboratory in Alais, in the south of France. Alais was considered the unofficial capital of the French silkworm industry. No sooner had he begun working with the silkworms than he received a message that his father was ill. By the time he arrived in Arbois, his father was dead. His death was just the beginning. During the following year, the Pasteurs would lose two more daughters to typhoid fever: Camille at age two and Cecile at age twelve.

There was no time for mourning or grief. Pasteur kept both at bay by concentrating on the silk growers and the problem of pebrine. He returned to Alais and began studying silkworms under the microscope. He noticed that infected silkworms were full of spots, which he called corpuscles. The greater the number of corpuscles a silkworm had, the sicker it was. From his research, he had learned that some scientists thought the corpuscles were the source of the disease.

Pasteur first wanted to know if pebrine was contagious. He placed sick silkworms on mulberry leaves, their favorite food. He then fed healthy silkworms the same leaves from which the sick ones had eaten. Soon after, the healthy silkworms developed corpuscles and died.

Pasteur also learned that if a silkworm egg contained corpuscles, the larva that developed from the egg also contained corpuscles. He believed that halting the spread of pebrine started with the egg. He advised the silkworm growers to separate diseased silkworm eggs from healthy ones and destroy the diseased eggs. To determine which eggs were diseased, he told the silk growers to check for corpuscles in both moth parents by examining them under the microscope. If no corpuscles were found in either parent, the egg was healthy and could be cultivated.

Confident that his method of separating the eggs would halt the spread of pebrine, Pasteur returned to Paris to the École Normale to cultivate his own set of silkworm eggs. However, he had still not discovered the reason for the souring wine, so he also returned to his fermentation studies. Like a juggler with many balls in the air at the same time, Pasteur juggled research on two scientific problems simultaneously.

Pasteur was determined to find a way to keep the wines from going sour without changing their flavor. He set up a laboratory in Arbois, the city of his childhood. He observed many different wines under the microscope. He had shown in his work with the spoiled beet juice that the wrong kind of microorganisms caused it to sour. He theorized that the same thing was happening with the wine. How, then, could he kill the microorganisms before they caused the wine to ferment? He tried adding antiseptics to the wine, but they made it taste worse than it did from normal souring. Day and night he thought about this problem. Finally, a simple answer came to him. The wines should be heated. The bacteria causing the acetic acid fermentation would be killed by the heat before they could turn the wine to acid.

Pasteur experimented with different heat times and temperatures. He learned that he could heat the wines up to 55 degrees Celsius (131 degrees Fahrenheit) and not harm their flavor or aroma. That temperature would kill the bacteria that were causing the wine to turn sour.

All important scientific discoveries are accompanied by controversy, and this one was no exception. Pasteur did not have long to wait for the arguments to begin. The vintners were against heating the wines. They did not believe Pasteur when he claimed heat would do no harm. Pasteur fought back with scientific fact. Microorganisms caused the bad fermentations and needed to be killed to save the wine. He gave people heated and unheated wine to drink. He challenged them to find a difference between the two. "These additional testings eliminated the last doubt as to the improvement of wine through heating," he wrote.[8] Gradually, the French people, not just the wine growers, came to realize that Pasteur was right. His method of heating wine to prevent it from souring spread to other wine-producing countries. Not only was Pasteur a hero in France, winegrowers throughout the world considered him a hero as well.

Pasteur's method of using heat to destroy microorganisms became known as pasteurization. In time, pasteurization was also proven to be beneficial to the dairy and beer industries.

Pasteur had no time to savor his success with wine. He had to continue to work on the silkworm disease. When he traveled to Alais in the spring of 1866, the silkworm growers met him with hostility. He was supposed to be a knowledgeable scientist. He had disproven spontaneous generation, found anaerobic bacteria, and saved the French wine industry. But his method of selecting healthy eggs had not helped the silk growers. They had followed Pasteur's directions precisely. They had discarded the eggs of moths that had corpuscles, and allowed only those free of them to grow. Pasteur's method had not worked. Even the larvae that had hatched from healthy eggs—larvae with no corpuscles at all—were becoming sick and dying.

Pasteur did not have an answer to the mystery of pebrine without corpuscles. He had seen the same thing happen to the larvae he had grown from eggs in his laboratory. Instead of corpuscles, the healthy larvae had soft, flaccid bodies. Pasteur stayed in Alais until June, the end of the silkworm growing season. He worked day and night, asking himself the same question over and over again. Why did some silkworms that died of pebrine show corpuscles while others did not?

One day in 1867, in his laboratory in Alais, an odd thought about the silkworm mystery came to him. Perhaps the silkworms without corpuscles didn't have pebrine at all. Perhaps they were suffering from a separate disease altogether. That would provide a good explanation for why they had no corpuscles.

Pasteur's odd thought proved to be correct. There were two diseases of silkworms. Pebrine caused the silkworms to have corpuscles. The other disease, flacherie, did not.

Again Pasteur buried himself in his lab. The methods he had devised for fighting pebrine—examining eggs under the microscope for corpuscles—worked when the crop of silkworms had pebrine alone. Pasteur studied the silkworms with flacherie and saw that they contained bacteria in their intestines. He showed the silkworm growers how to cut out the intestine of a silkworm, mix it with water, and examine it under a microscope. Test a sampling of silkworms for the bacteria, Louis instructed them. If there

At the request of Emperor Napoléon III, Pasteur studied the diseases of silkworms. After much scientific study and observation, Pasteur realized that silkworms were showing signs of two separate diseases – pebrine and flacherie. Pasteur's diligent observations saved the French silkworm industry.

are no bacteria present in the intestines of the sample, the entire crop of silkworms is safe to grow. Pasteur had found ways for the silkworm growers to combat both pebrine and flacherie.

In 1867, Pasteur resigned his position at École Normale and became a professor of chemistry at the Sorbonne. The same year, he accepted an invitation to visit Napoléon III and Empress Eugénie at their palace in Compiègne. Pasteur spent much of the visit talking about science to his hosts and their guests, who were very impressed by his research. A year later, when the French government refused to approve the building of a new laboratory for Pasteur, the emperor ordered one to be constructed in the garden of the École Normale. He even contributed 30,000 francs of his personal money to the project.

The scientific battles over silkworms and wine that Pasteur had so fiercely fought and won came at a cost to his health. On the morning of October 19, 1868, Pasteur felt a strange prickling sensation on his left side. He ignored it and went to work as usual in his laboratory, but took to his bed in the afternoon after he began to shake uncontrollably. He was still not feeling well in the evening, but he insisted on keeping a commitment to address the French Academy of Sciences. Later that night, after he had gone to bed, the prickling sensation returned. He was not able to speak. He had suffered a cerebral hemorrhage, or a stroke. This occurs when brain tissue does not receive enough blood because a vessel has become blocked or broken. Depending upon where in the brain this happens, the results can be paralysis and difficulty speaking.

Pasteur's condition improved over the next day, then again worsened, but he never lost consciousness. On October 21, Dr. Godelier, his personal physician, noted, "Active mind. Would have liked to talk science."[9] During the times he was able to speak, Pasteur begged the doctor to cut off his paralyzed arm. "It is like lead; if only it could be cut off," he cried.[10] After a week of suffering, during which his wife and children were sure he was going to die, Pasteur began to get well.

Soon he was once again talking of the laboratory and his experiments to the parade of well-known scientists who sat at his bedside and encouraged his recovery. That following January, Pasteur had recovered enough to travel to Alais in time for the start of the silkworm growing season. His left arm was paralyzed and his left foot dragged when he walked. But he had survived the stroke. Like his battles with sour wine and silkworm disease, he had emerged a victor.

Typhoid Fever

Three of Pasteur's daughters died of typhoid fever, a common killer of the 1800s. Typhoid fever is rarely found today in the United States, but it still threatens many developing countries worldwide. It is caused by the bacterium Salmonella typhi, also known as Eberthella typhosa and Bacillus typhosus. This bacterium was discovered in 1880 by two independent German physicians, Karl Eberth and Robert Koch. Salmonella typhi is found only in humans. After infection, the bacteria move to the blood and intestinal tract. They are shed in the feces.

Karl Eberth

One of the ways a person can get typhoid fever is by consuming contaminated food or drink. Another way is by drinking water or washing vegetables in water that has been contaminated by sewage containing Salmonella typhi.

A high fever is the first sign that a person has contracted typhoid fever. Stomachaches, headaches, loss of appetite, and feeling weak are also signs of the disease. The bacteria multiply in the liver and spleen, which often become enlarged. A rosy rash is sometimes seen on the trunk of the infected person's body. A person who thinks he has typhoid fever can have his stool and blood samples tested for the presence of the bacteria. Typhoid fever is treatable with antibiotics, which were not available in the nineteenth century. Left untreated, the disease can cause death.

Patients who survive a bout of typhoid fever will continue to carry the bacteria in their bodies even after their symptoms are gone. They are considered carriers because they are still capable of transmitting the disease to others. Typhoid fever survivors may remain in a carrier stage for years. Some become lifelong carriers. Frequent hand washing, among other things, will help lessen the chances of a carrier giving the disease to others.

After his rabies vaccine proved to be successful, Pasteur asked the French Academy of Sciences to build a research center for rabies and microbiological research. The research center, named The Pasteur Institute, was opened in Paris in 1888. Pasteur served as director of the Pasteur Institute until his death in 1895. Over the years, many scientists from the Pasteur Institute have received the Nobel Prize.

5

Disease Fighter

Pasteur was only forty-five years old when he suffered his stroke. For the remainder of his life, he would feel its affects in his movement and speech. Although the stroke slowed him down, it could not stop him. Pasteur continued to conduct scientific research with the help of laboratory assistants.

In 1870, France went to war with Prussia. Louis, Marie, and their surviving daughter, Marie-Louise, fled to Arbois. Jean-Baptiste, their son, joined the French army. Louis tried to enlist as well, but was turned down because of his age and health. He showed his national pride in his own way: he returned an honorary doctor of medicine degree awarded him by the University of Bonn in 1868.

In 1871, Germany defeated the French army. The fiercely patriotic scientist took France's defeat hard. His entire life's work had been devoted to improving the lives of the French people. One of the ways he could continue to help his countrymen was with his knowledge of fermentation. He used it to improve the quality of French beer so that it rivaled its German counterpart.

Each research project Pasteur worked on made the relationship between germs and illness clearer. He continued to study fermentation until 1877, but his interest, increasingly, turned to disease and its prevention. He had lost three children to typhoid fever. He took to heart the fact that all his knowledge of microbes and germs had not been able to save them.

Great strides were made in the overall understanding of disease during the latter part of the nineteenth century. By then Pasteur was convinced that the only way to fight disease was to get rid of germs. One of the places that had the most germs was the very place people went to get well—the hospital. Doctors and nurses went from patient to patient without washing their hands. Sometimes they even used the same surgical instrument on several patients. Hospital wards were not cleaned properly, and bandages and bedclothes were seldom changed.

Pasteur implored doctors to begin using more sanitary measures, but most laughed at him. He was just a chemist, they said. What did he know about medicine? However, one Scottish doctor, Joseph Lister, began to put some of Pasteur's ideas to the test at his hospital in Edinburgh. Within two years he saw deaths of surgery patients decline from 95 percent to 15 percent. "It would afford me the highest gratification to show you how greatly surgery is indebted to you," Lister wrote to Pasteur.[1]

Pasteur made many more contributions to the study of disease. In 1880 he discovered a vaccine for chicken cholera, the scourge of poultry farmers that killed 90 percent of their flocks when it struck a farm. Pasteur took bacteria from a chicken that had died of cholera and grew it in a culture in his lab. Then he injected a small amount of the cultured bacteria into a sample of chickens. They became mildly sick, but shortly recovered. He then injected the same chickens with lethal dosages of chicken cholera bacteria. Instead of dying they remained healthy. In 1881, using the same method, Pasteur developed a vaccine against anthrax, a disease of cattle and sheep that can spread to humans. And in 1885, he successfully prevented rabies in Joseph Meister after the young boy had been bitten by a rabid dog. In appreciation, in 1888, the French government built Pasteur a research center. The Pasteur Institute is today one of the most respected centers of scientific research in all of Europe.

On December 27, 1892, a national holiday was declared in honor of Pasteur's seventieth birthday. A party was held at the Sorbonne. Public figures and scientists from around the world attended.

Pasteur spent his last years in quiet research at the Pasteur Institute and relaxing in the village of his childhood, Arbois. He suffered two small strokes in 1887. Toward the very end of his life, he was bedridden and unable to speak. He died on September 28, 1895, at seventy-two years of age. After a state funeral at the Cathedral of Notre Dame in Paris, Pasteur was laid to rest in a crypt beneath the Pasteur Institute. Even in death, he would not be far from his beloved scientific research.

Louis Pasteur has been described in many ways. Stephen Paget, a medical and historical writer, once wrote that Pasteur was "the most perfect man who has ever entered the Kingdom of Science."[2] Pasteur has also been called the father of modern medicine, the founder of bacteriology, and the father of microbiology. However he is remembered, it is because Pasteur spent his life fighting disease that immeasurable others have been able to enjoy their lives.

Although Louis Pasteur lived over one hundred years ago, he is still a large part of our everyday world. The next time you pour yourself a glass of milk, take a look at the word *pasteurized* right there on the carton. That one word tells you that the milk you are about to drink is safe. It is free from harmful microorganisms like bacteria, and it will not make you sick. You can thank Louis Pasteur for that.

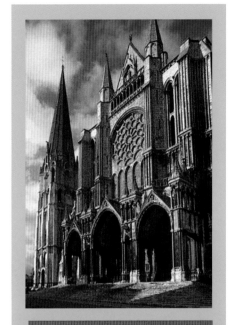

Notre Dame in Paris, the site of Pasteur's funeral.

The Pasteur Institute

The Pasteur Institute

The vaccination against rabies of young Joseph Meister in 1885 was so successful that Louis Pasteur asked the French Academy of Sciences for a research facility. Pasteur wanted the building to be the center for rabies research and microbiological research. He also wanted the facility to be a place where researchers could receive special training in the microbiological sciences.

The Pasteur Institute opened on November 14, 1888. The newspapers called it "The Rabies Palace." Pasteur was unable to speak that day, although he was present for the inaugural ceremony. His son, Jean-Baptiste, read his words:

"Always cultivate the spirit of criticism. Once it has been allowed to fail there is nothing to awaken an idea, nothing to stimulate great things. Without it, nothing will hold up."[3]

Louis Pasteur headed the Pasteur Institute until his death in 1895. The Pasteur Institute rose to become France's most prestigious scientific institute. Over the years eight scientists from the institute have been honored with Nobel Prizes.

In the early 1980s, a new disease that attacked the immune system was reported in the United States and other countries. It had been named Acquired Immune Deficiency Syndrome, or AIDS for short. Research teams in both the United States and France began to seriously study the virus. In late 1982, a team of virologists at the Pasteur Institute, headed by Luc Montagnier, Jean-Claude Chermann, and Françoise Barre-Sinoussi, began searching for the cause of the disease. Shortly thereafter, they reported the discovery of a new virus, which they called lymphaden-opathy-associated virus, or LAV. This is now known to be the AIDS-causing Human Immunodeficiency Virus (HIV). The Pasteur Institute team published their findings in May 1983 in _Science_. Other scientists at the Pasteur Institute developed a blood test for the disease, which was released in 1985. The Pasteur Institute continues to be one of the most respected scientific institutions in the world. By focusing on biochemistry, microbiology, and virology (the study of viruses), researchers there continue to make many advances in the study of AIDS and other diseases.

Chronology

1822	Louis Pasteur is born in Dole, France, on December 27
1827	The Pasteur family moves to Arbois
1838	Louis Pasteur leaves to study in Paris, but homesickness brings him back to Arbois within a few weeks
1840	Receives bachelor of letters degree from Collège Royal de Besançon
1842	Receives bachelor of science degree from Collège Royal de Besançon
1843	Enters École Normale Supérieure in Paris to study for doctoral degree
1844	Begins studying crystals
1847	Discovers the reason for differences in the polarization of light in tartaric and paratartaric acids; receives doctor of science degree
1848	Joins National Guard; mother dies
1849	Becomes a professor of chemistry at University of Strasbourg; marries Marie Laurent
1853	Receives the Legion of Honor medal
1854	Accepts position of dean and professor of chemistry at the University of Lille
1857	Presents his findings on alcoholic fermentation to the Academy of Sciences; begins a ten-year term as director of scientific studies at École Normale
1859	Daughter, Jeanne, dies of typhoid fever at age twelve
1860	Receives Prize for Experimental Physiology from Academy of Sciences
1861	Discovers anaerobic bacteria
1862	Is elected to the Academy of Sciences in the mineralogy section
1864	The Academy of Sciences accepts Pasteur's findings that disprove theory of spontaneous generation; Pasteur theorizes that disease is caused by germs—he calls this the germ theory of disease
1865	Begins a fifteen-year study on diseases of silkworms; begins studies on fermentation, which will yield the process of pasteurization
1866	Daughters Camille, age two, and Cecile, age twelve, die of typhoid fever
1867	Becomes professor of chemistry at the Sorbonne in Paris
1868	Suffers his first stroke
1880	Discovers a vaccine for chicken cholera
1881	Proves anthrax vaccine protects against the disease in cattle
1885	Gives the first series of rabies vaccines to a nine-year-old boy
1887	Suffers two strokes
1888	The Pasteur Institute is opened; Louis Pasteur becomes its first director and remains so until his death
1895	Dies on September 28

Timeline of Discovery

460 B.C.	Hippocrates is born. He is the first person to recognize medicine as a science.
A.D. 1546	Girolamo Fracastoro studies contagion and determines infections can be passed in three ways: by direct contact, by contact with contaminated articles and through the air.
1674	Antoni van Leeuwenhoek is the first to observe microscopic life when he examines a drop of lake water under his improved microscope.
1796	Edward Jenner performs first smallpox inoculation on an eight-year-old boy.
1840s	Several European doctors and one American, Dr. Oliver Wendell Holmes, recognize the contagious nature of childbed fever, also known as puerperal fever or puerperal sepsis, a disease that killed new mothers. Louis Pasteur would discover the responsible infectious agent, *Streptococcus pyogenes,* in 1879.
1859	Louis Pasteur proves the theory of spontaneous generation is incorrect using flasks with necks shaped like the letter S. His experiments paved the way for the germ theory of disease.
1865	Joseph Lister is the first physician to use a disinfectant to kill the growth of bacteria on wounds.
1876	Robert Koch discovers that the infective agent of anthrax, a disease of cattle, is a rodlike bacterium.
1880	Robert Koch and Karl Eberth, separately, discover the bacterium that causes typhoid fever.
1882	Robert Koch discovers the bacterium that causes tuberculosis.
1885	Louis Pasteur successfully performs the first rabies vaccination.
1913	Béla Schick develops a test for diphtheria.
1952	Jonas Salk develops a vaccine against poliomyelitis.
1970	The first rubella vaccine is produced by a Belgian subsidiary of an American pharmaceutical company.
1983	Researchers in France and the United States co-discover the Human Immunodeficiency Virus (HIV), which causes AIDS.
2005	Amid much controversy, human stem cells are studied as a possible means of treating and curing disease.

Chapter Notes

Chapter 1
A Prepared Mind
1. Pasteur Vallery-Radot, *Louis Pasteur* (New York: Alfred A. Knopf, 1970), p. 176.

Chapter 2
A Boy in Arbois
1. Patrice Debré, *Louis Pasteur*, translated by Elborg Forster (Baltimore: Johns Hopkins University, 1998), p. 140.
2. Pasteur Vallery-Radot, *Louis Pasteur* (New York: Alfred A. Knopf, 1970), p. 12.
3. Debré, p. 9.
4. Vallery-Radot, p.14.
5. Hilaire Cuny, *Louis Pasteur: The Man and His Theories* (New York: Paul S. Eriksson, Inc., 1966), p. 28.
6. Debré, p. 15.
7. Ibid., p. 19.

Chapter 3
A Chemist by Training
1. Patrice Debré, *Louis Pasteur*, translated by Elborg Forster (Baltimore: Johns Hopkins University, 1998), p. 23.
2. Ibid., p. 33.
3. Pasteur Vallery-Radot, *Louis Pasteur* (New York: Alfred A. Knopf, 1970), p. 34.
4. Debré, p. 42.
5. Vallery-Radot, 25.
6. Ibid., p. 8.
7. Ibid., p. 30.

8. Gerald L. Geison, *The Private Science of Louis Pasteur* (Princeton: Princeton University Press, 1995), p. 25.
9. Vallery-Radot, p. 39.

Chapter 4
Wines and Worms
1. Pasteur Vallery-Radot, *Louis Pasteur* (New York: Alfred A. Knopf, 1970), p. 39.
2. Hilaire Cuny, *Louis Pasteur: The Man and His Theories*, translated by Patrick Evens (New York: Paul S. Eriksson, Inc., 1966), p. 28.
3. Patrice Debré, *Louis Pasteur*, translated by Elborg Forster (Baltimore: Johns Hopkins University, 1998), p. 1.
4. Debré, p. 57.
5. Vallery-Radot, p. 58.
6. Debré, p. 161.
7. René Dubos, *Louis Pasteur: Free Lance of Science* (New York: Da Capo Press, 1986), p. 177.
8. Debré, p. 237.
9. Ibid., p. 209.
10. Vallery-Radot, p. 106.

Chapter 5
Disease Fighter
1. René Dubos, *Louis Pasteur: Free Lance of Science* (New York: Da Capo Press, 1986), p. 246.
2. Ibid., p. 24.
3. Patrice Debré, *Louis Pasteur*, translated by Elborg Forster (Baltimore: Johns Hopkins University, 1998), p. 472.

Glossary

cultivate (KUL-te-vate)—to grow.

culture (KUL-chur)—to grow microorganisms in a prepared dish.

fermentation (fur-men-TAY-shun)—the process of changing sugar into alcohol and carbon dioxide gas.

germ (jurm)—a microbe that causes disease.

germ theory of disease (jurm THEAR-ee of dis-EEZ)—Pasteur's theory that microscopic germs cause disease.

hypothesis (hi-POTH-a-sis)—a scientific guess.

immunity (im-YOON-i-tee)—protection from disease.

inoculate (in-KNOCK-u-late)—to give a vaccination.

metabolism (me-TAB-o-lizm)—the processes of a living organism.

microbe (MY-krobe)—a microorganism.

microorganism (MY-kro-or-gah-nizm)—a living thing that can be seen only under a microscope.

pasteurization (past-chur-iz-AY-chun)—the process invented by Louis Pasteur of heating wine, milk, or other beverage to a certain temperature for a set amount of time in order to kill harmful bacteria and other microbes.

polarize (POLE-er-ize)—to cause light to rotate in one direction.

rabies (RAY-bees)—a potentially deadly disease that is passed through the bite of an infected animal.

sanitary (SAN-i-ter-ee)—free from germs.

spontaneous generation (spon-TAY-nee-ous gen-er-AY-shun)—the theory that life can arise from nonliving matter; Pasteur disproved this theory.

tanner (tan-er)—a person who turns the hides of animals into leather.

vaccination (vax-sin-AY-shun)—a dose of weakened microbes given to a patient in order to build up immunity to a particular disease.

vintner (VINT-ner)—a person who makes wine.

yeast (YEEST)—a microorganism that aids the process of fermentation.

For Further Reading

Books

Ackerman, Jane. *Louis Pasteur and the Founding of Microbiology.* Greensboro, N.C.: Morgan Reynolds Publishing, 2004.

Alphin, Elaine Marie. *Germ Hunter: A Story About Louis Pasteur.* Minneapolis: Carolrhoda Books, 2004.

Burton, M. J. *Louis Pasteur: Founder of Microbiology.* New York: Franklin Watts, 2000.

Fullick, Anne. *Louis Pasteur.* Chicago: Heinemann, 2002.

Gogerly, Liz. *Scientists Who Made History.* London: Hodder and Stoughton Children's Division, 2002.

Parker, Steve. *Louis Pasteur and Germs.* Broomhall, Penn.: Chelsea House, 1995.

Smith, Linda Wasmer. *Louis Pasteur: Disease Fighter.* Berkeley Heights, N.J.: Enslow Publishers, Inc., 1997.

Thomson, Pat. *The Silkworm Mystery: The Story of Louis Pasteur.* New York: Simon and Schuster, 1997.

Works Consulted

Cuny, Hilaire. *Pasteur: The Man and His Theories.* Translated by Patrick Evans. New York: Paul S. Eriksson, Inc., 1966.

Debré, Patrice. *Louis Pasteur.* Translated by Elborg Forster. Baltimore: Johns Hopkins University Press, 1998.

Dubos, René. *Louis Pasteur: Free Lance of Science.* New York: Da Capo Press, 1986.

Geison, Gerald L. *The Private Science of Louis Pasteur.* Princeton: Princeton University Press, 1995.

Vallery-Radot, Pasteur. *Louis Pasteur.* New York: Alfred A. Knopf, 1970.

On the Internet

Access Excellence-The National Health Museum: *The Slow Death of Spontaneous Generation (1668–1859),* by Russell Levine and Chris Evers, © 1994–2004
http://
www.accessexcellence.org/RC/
AB/BC/
Spontaneous_Generation.html

National Inventors Hall of Fame: *Louis Pasteur*
http://www.invent.org/
hall_of_fame/119.html

The Nobel Prize: *The Pasteur Institute,* by François Jacob, translated by Louise Ratford
http://www.nobel.se/medicine/
articles/jacob/

Index